Louie the Miracle Elephant

Written by
Grandma Marian

Illustrated by
Vanessa Snyder

For Lauren,
with love,
Grandma Marian

For Aaron, Joey,
Rach, Liz, Cam,
Eli, Aaron Jr., and Ana,
V.

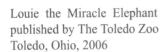

Louie the Miracle Elephant
published by The Toledo Zoo
Toledo, Ohio, 2006

ISBN number: 0-977697401

Library of Congress
Control Number: 2005911341

Printed by Promus Printing (China) Co., Ltd

6/08
E
05

Do you like the zoo as much as I do,
Watching monkeys and zebras and that big horned gnu?
Polar bears swim and snakes sleep in the sun,
While a pair of chimpanzees entertain everyone.

Most animals there come from lands far away,
But a few were born there, and most of them stay.
Our new baby, Louie,
Is my favorite now.
He has stolen my heart,
And I'll tell you how.

1

He's among the first elephants born in a zoo
Through science and skill; it's really quite new.
That's why they say he's a miracle child.
It never could happen in the African wild.

Oh, they tried and they tried the regular way
With Jack, the big male and the female, Rene'.

See, the female has eggs and the male plants his sperm
Inside the female, to wiggle and squirm.

'Till it gets to her eggs, when the two become one,
And that is just how a child's life is begun!

egg   sperm

But Rene' didn't care for Jack's loving advances;
She wasn't prepared for Savanna romances.
If that elephant Jack tried to hug her and kiss her
She would push him away,
So his kisses would miss her!

It soon became clear to the boss of the zoo
That he needed some help, so he said to his crew,
"To have Rene's baby would be very nice,
But it just isn't working, so I need your advice."
He talked and discussed with each woman and man.
In the end they made up a most wonderful plan!

They had figured a way to get sperm from the male
And keep it quite cool so it wouldn't get stale.
Then they'd go to Rene and put the sperm in.
And hope that a new elephant's life would begin.

Imagine the mountains of work that it took!
The study and planning could fill a big book!
It had to be done at just the right time,
So the sperm would arrive to the egg in its prime.

Well the day finally came. They were ready to start.
There were doctors and keepers, each one had a part.

As Rene' was brought in, doctors gathered around
To check and make sure she was healty and sound.

They put the sperm in with caution and care.
This had only been done once or twice anywhere!

7

Then calmly she walked
To the pond for a drink,
As she left I could see her
Right eye give a wink!

She is quite clever. I think that she knew
Exactly what humans were aiming to do.

8

Several weeks would go by
Before people would know
If a baby elephant
Had started to grow.

Rene' spent her days
Just playing and eating,
Waving her trunk
To give tourists a greeting.

9

It was finally time. The people were tense.
No wonder! For weeks they had been in suspense!
Did the sperm find the egg? Was their plan a success?
When the doctors examine, will their answer be "Yes!!?"
They checked Rene' closely, not too slow or too fast.
And then they announced, "She's pregnant at last!"

"Hurray and hurrah!"
The crew shouted with glee,
But Rene' lumbered off
To eat leaves off a tree.

She wasn't impressed
Or even excited,
But all of the humans
Were simply delighted.

There was much work to be done.
They had to prepare
And be sure that Rene'
Would be getting good care.

The doctors made certain
Her diet was right.
No more fatty foods,
Not even one bite!

No meat, just alfalfa, veggies and hay
And gallons of water she drank every day.
They made a big bag of sweet hay hanging high
To make her trunk stretch as she reached for the sky!
What a comical sight, when Rene', down below,
Tried to get at that hay as it swung to and fro.

13

To be sure she kept active, they walked her alot,
And she rolled in the mud when the weather was hot.
They bathed her each day to relieve any stress,
So her handlers could handle her better, I guess.

14

I must tell you now, it's important to mention
It was more than Rene' that needed attention.
Two elephant nurseries, nothing like yours,
Were built for the baby, inside and outdoors.

A pool was designed where the baby could drink,
And not get its foot or its head stuck, I think.
Even the floors were made skid-proof and rough
To keep him from falling or that kind of stuff.

An elephant baby grows for almost two years
Inside its mother 'till the birthing time nears.

In the middle of April, they examined Rene'
And found that her baby was due any day!
They started to watch her all day and all night.
The crew never let her get out of their sight.

Then finally that month, on the thirtieth day,
The baby began to come out of Rene'.

The people were tense. It was taking so long!
What would they do if something went wrong?

When one leg came out, Rene' rolled on her side,
Oh my! Could it be that the baby had died?

But they tied up that leg,
Just as quick as a wink,
And they pulled on the rope,
And what do you think?

The baby slid out, very healthy and hale
On one end a trunk, on the other a tail.

He was tipsy, and wobbling
All over the place,
Didn't know what to do
With that trunk on his face!

René' tried to feed him like a cow feeds her calf,
But what happened next made everyone laugh!
Poor thing didn't know the right way to nurse
And his long pesky trunk made everything worse!

He had to be taught to keep his trunk quiet
And drink René's milk, so good for his diet.
But he finally learned, and soon ate with no trouble.
He got so much milk that his size seemed to double!

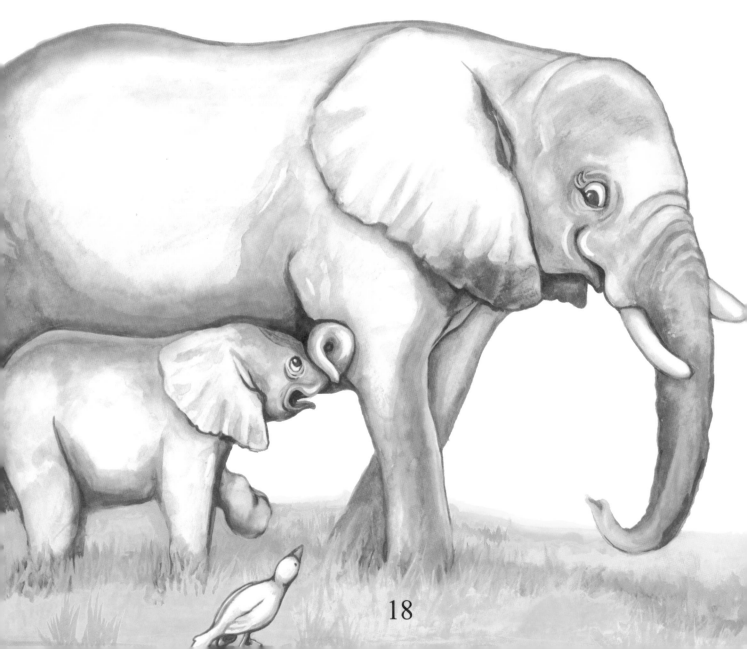

18

Young Louie was curious.
He raced all around,
Examining each wonderful
Thing that he found.

One day he got stuck
On a log that was there!
His front on one side,
His behind in mid-air!

19

Holiday times are always great fun,
For Louie knows how to amuse everyone.

At Halloween season, the folks at the zoo
Fill huge balls with popcorn for Louie to chew.
Bright boxes of fruit all wrapped up with care
And pumpkins and cabbages placed here and there.

He stomps on the boxes
And throws them away.
It makes people smile
To see Loiue play!

Sometimes he walks backwards
To get a good start,
Then, full speed ahead,
He breaks things apart!

21

eeeuh!

Louie enjoys
Entertaining the crowd.
He even rears up
And he bellows outloud.

22

With a very mischievous
Smile on his face,
He throws trunkfulls of popcorn
All over the place.

Then he eats all his veggies
And fruit, every bite.
Keeps playing and eating!
My, my what a sight!

23

When he got into mischief,
His mom made it clear
He would not be allowed
To be rough and tough here!

In elephant language,
She scolded her son,
But he was confused.
He was just having fun!

24

Easter brings eggs
Made of paper-mache'
Filled up with food
That he eats right away.

25

The season of Christmas
Is special, he knows.
It's more than the gifts
Wrapped with ribbons and bows.

It's also the families
Who come day and night
To hear their sweet laughter
Fills him with delight.

26

But life's not just play,
So when Christmas is gone,
The process of learning has to go on.

Young Louie has lessons, just like any kid,
He had to learn manners, and learn them he did.

He holds Rene's tail, when they go for a walk,
And she teaches him things, in elephant talk.

Each day when it's bath time,
He lies on each side.
It feels, oh so good
When they're scrubbing his hide!

When mealtime is near, he has learned self control.
He is told, "Pick it up!" and he picks up his bowl!
He waits while it's filled with his favorite snack,
And when he's through eating, he puts his bowl back!

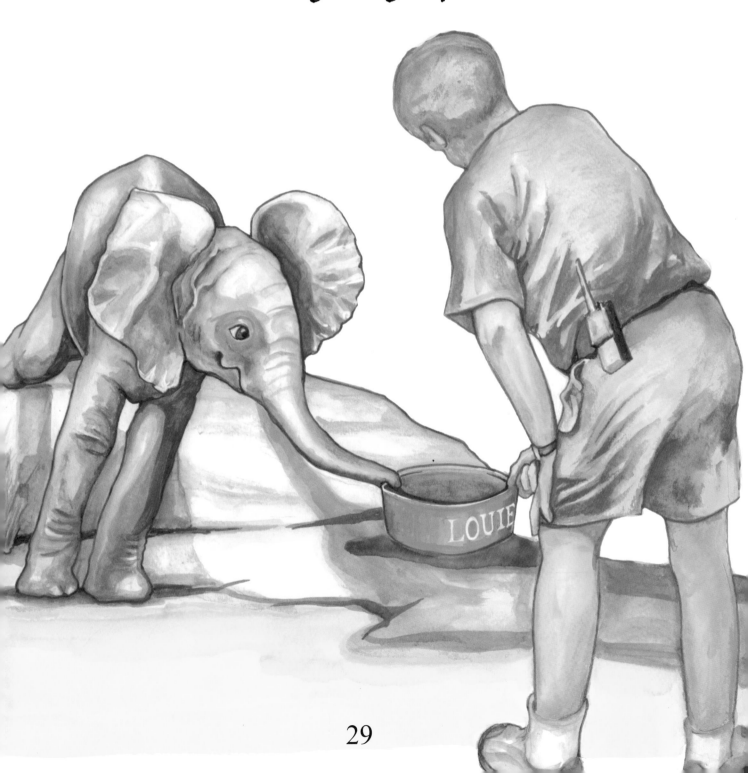

And now he's an artist!
It's his latest success,
Though he's covered with paint
And looks quite a mess.

I'm simply amazed
At what Louie can do
And almost as proud
As your folks are of you!

30

I could tell you much more
About Louie, my friend,
But if I did that,
Then this book wouldn't end!

"Portrait"

"Let's Play!"

"A Walk with Mom"

Louie's
Scrap
Book

31

Come see for yourself,
As Louie grows taller,
Some day, next to him,
His mom will be smaller!